88

POWERFUL
AFFIRMATIONS

Kayon Beckford

88

POWERFUL
AFFIRMATIONS

Kayon Beckford

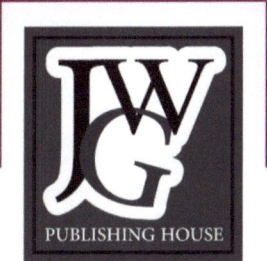

JWG
PUBLISHING HOUSE

JWG Publishing

ISBN: 978-1-7345938-9-1

Cover Design:
Business Start-up & Marketing Solutions LLC
and JWG Publishing House

For information please visit
www.kayonbeckford.com
478-353-5081
affirmationsforyouu@gmail.com

Published by

JWG Publishing
Printed in the United States of America.

DEDICATION

Amidst the darkness my Lord and Savior showed
me the light and to Him I dedicate this book. To
my family and friends who have supported, loved
believed and encouraged me; who have traveled this
journey alongside me, and; to all my readers my
hope is that you find peace as you read along.

Peace, love and light.

A kind or encouraging word can act as a moment of
great solace to the downhearted. Remember God is
Love, so Love Always.

INTRODUCTION

Like all other years before, we thought that 2020 would bring us joy and new wonderful life experiences, but I guess we can't always get what we wish for. The Coronavirus Disease 2019 took us by surprise and the domino effect has been extensive. The stress and duress of it all can have and has had damaging results on us. Daily news of the continuous rise in number of deaths and infections due to the lackadaisicalness and foolhardy nature of our people continues to pour over our mass media. It has literally broken me spiritually, mentally and physically. Unbelievable as it is, I found passion in writing down my deepest thoughts during this time, especially due to the COVID-19 Pandemic.

I had to find some way to rise above the uncertainty with clear understanding knowing that there is always that light at the end of every dark tunnel. Many of us as human beings may have different levels of uncertainty whether it's suffering from anxiety or even depression. There are even times in our lives where we feel that the overwhelming pressure is far too great to bear. There are moments, as simple as they may be, we need encouragement just to brighten our days. Whatever the need, positivity is a welcomed factor in all situations. Oftentimes, all we need are a few words to lift our spirit. I now have the ability to share my deepest thoughts and beliefs with each and every one of you. This book gave me a voice that allows me to bring out my definite purpose of my life by adding value not only to myself but to others as well.

It is my hope that that through my 'voice' I am able to offer some form of healing or means of solace in these trying times. Never forget that God is able to do all things, and with him by our side, we can overcome all trials and tribulations. Having a belief system that is driven by faith is a remarkable feeling which brings me to a verse that will always live within me. Philippians 4:13 " I can do all things through Christ who strengthens me".

POWERFUL
AFFIRMATIONS

Never spend so much time
focusing on others that you miss
out on the moments that you
created for yourself.

Manifest abundance over your
life and keep your dreams
close to your heart. Focus on
the prize; avoid looking to the
left or right, and let faith be the
compass to guide you in the
direction that you should go.

Be thankful for the small blessings in life by being humble; it changes your attitude. Gratefulness will allow you to embrace more, and you will be better able to receive and appreciate the bigger things that are yet to come.

Love and respect go a very long way. Know your worth. Never allow anyone to diminish your self-worth.

As long as you have the Father,
you will not live a limited
life. Remove lack and limiting
thoughts from your mind. Your
thoughts create realities. Step
into your greatness and live the
life that you desire!

Life is about making moments
count and enjoying the
experiences. Live it joyfully and
purposefully.

Until you stop being consumed by the ugliness in others, you will continue to rob yourself of the beauty within you.

Permit yourself to be one of a kind, created in the image and likeness of God. Know who you are and be true to yourself. You are a masterpiece and a divine true expression of God. Take center stage, be a star and walk in your power with no apology.

Accept who you are. Remember where you have been; but most importantly, know where you want to be.

Kindness makes you the most beautiful person in the world. Show it, spread it and sprinkle it!!

Whatever is for you will manifest. Keep planting your seed and watering your garden. Never stop until it blooms.

Never think that what you have to offer is insignificant. There's someone out there who really needs it. You can always find value and inspiration in someone else's story.

Life does whatever is necessary to mold us into shape and prepare us for greatness. It may not look or feel this way, because what we experience in life may seem difficult, painful, and unnecessary.

You deserve whatever good comes your way; you are inspired, and you have the power to accomplish everything you need today. Everything that you need is being supplied.

What are you willing to sacrifice to have what you want and to be where you want to be? That is your greatest challenge.

What you have done is nothing compared to what you can do. Just know that you are capable of more than what you can see.

Your story doesn't define who you are. How you evolve in the end, after all the adversity, is what defines you.

Focus on being positive, because the thoughts you think and words you speak are powerful.

You are in complete control
of your success in life. Take
a risk and make a change; do
something you would never dare
to do.

Your twists and turns don't
mean that your life is over. God
allows you to be triumphant;
you have an established end set
by our Father, and nothing can
change that.

Use the power of now to get to where you want to go. Your potential is limitless; step into your greatness without apology. It doesn't matter what people say; step out and play big.

Don't allow anyone or any circumstance to devalue you. At any moment in time you have the opportunity to reset. Declare that you are worthy!

Nothing happens until you move. Take a step today and do something. Use what you have now to create what you want tomorrow.

It doesn't matter if the glass is half full or half empty; be grateful that you have a glass and that there is something in it.

Respect yourself enough to walk away from anything that no longer serves you.

Plenty of people miss their share of happiness - not because they didn't find it, but because they didn't stop to enjoy it. Happiness is a choice, not a result. It can only come from you.

Gratitude can turn a negative into a positive. Find a way to be thankful for your troubles so they can become your blessings.

Step outside of the box
and learn to be different.
You never know what you
can do in life until you try.
Don't be complacent.

Never worry about the
closed doors. Look ahead
and make room for the
new doors to open for you.
Keep moving.

Don't allow yourself to get caught up with people and things that you cannot change. Instead, let go and focus on the things that you can change - the things that will enhance your life to make you a better you. Remember, you deserve to be happy.

Challenge yourself that no matter what life throws your way, you are going to stay calm and in peace. All the forces of darkness cannot keep you from your destiny.

What you do in your defining moment will either make you or break you. Your character, your integrity, and how you treat people is what will carry you towards your legacy.

Never let anyone tell you that your idea or dream is impossible. Keep a clear mind and focus on your goals.

Confidence is believing in yourself. Confidence is knowing who you were designed to be. Believe in it and you will walk taller and smile bigger. You will feel irresistible and amazing.

Sometimes life doesn't give you what you want; not because you don't deserve it, but because you deserve more.

Today, take a deep breath; release with gratitude. Say a prayer and thank God in advance for the blessing that will take place in your life today.

Soon, when this period of your life comes to an end, you are going to look back and be THANKFUL that you never gave up.

When you are going through things, you have to grow through it. You have to face it head-on. Face your fear in every single way; as long as you know you can do it, then it doesn't matter what people say.

The power of being great
has to come from within. It
doesn't matter the push or the
motivation you are given. You
have to permit yourself to be
great.

Let your light shine so bright
that it will never go out. Own
it, embrace it.
Permit others to shine too.
You don't need confirmation
or validation to be that
rainbow.

Sometimes things don't turn
out the way we planned.
Never give up; just stay
solid and you will come out
better than before.

Be thankful for what you
have and for what you
don't have, because there
is definitely a reason
for this. Be FOREVER
GRATEFUL.

You were created for greatness. Never let the obstacles of life get in your way. If you want it badly enough you have to go for it. Keep winning.

Whatever you are focusing on, or whatever you are giving energy to is what will happen. Act as if it's already happening.

Stop letting your past own you. Learn to create new experiences and write new chapters. Stop being a slave of your past.

Life is about having the courage to step out fearlessly. Have faith even when you don't see a way. Have the drive to keep going even when you feel like quitting.

Be so determined not to let hardships of life tear you apart. Instead, use that strength to go on to accomplish whatever you want. Life is filled with many challenges. Keep going; you can do it!

Let your character build by staying patient and trusting the journey. The best part of life is not surviving but thriving.

Don't be distracted by the drama. Be true to yourself and stay the course. Leave room for life to happen and always attract the good and lovely in your everyday life.

Dig your heels in and get your fire back. Don't allow yourself to get stuck in the middle. Keep on keeping on!

Your identity will determine your destiny. You will never know who you are until you discover who God made you to be. Walk in the purpose of your truth and you will be blessed from top to bottom.

You are strong - not by your own hands, but by the hands of God. He will hold you; He will comfort you, and He will supply all your needs. Just keep honoring Him. It may seem like forever but keep holding strong.

Don't ever allow the darkness
to take over the light in you.
Be blessed, be bold, and be
vibrant today as you take
on your challenges. Reflect
peace and love. Be FOREVER
GRATEFUL.

Don't ever let the doubters
deter you from your blessing!
You have worked too hard to
even entertain the thought.
Opposition will always be
present.

Know who you are; you know what you want, and you know that you can have it. Life and death are in the power of the tongue.

Sometimes you have to face the storm to help others get through it. We question ourselves and ask why; just know that God has a bigger and better plan for you.

Never throw in the towel just because you came face to face with the opposition. Take tiny steps if you have to and remember that those tiny steps will eventually turn out to be your huge jumps. Keep going; you can do it!!!

They will try everything to get your attention, but don't react to their drama. Keep a clean heart, say less, but pay attention. They will eventually see you rise. Things thrown at you will never reach you because you will be too far ahead.

Some people want to see you fail so they can sit back, relax and enjoy your failure. Smash the glass ceiling!!!!

Stay in your shine. Own what you are building and walk with grace and confidence. Without a doubt, things will eventually fall into place and work itself out in time.

Sometimes you have to hit rock bottom to know how strong you are. No matter how strong the trials and tribulations become, strengthen your wings, straighten your crown, and thank God that you were sustained through the trials.

Whatever they did to you, they did it to God. It doesn't matter how judgmental people are; just know that your purpose is much bigger than their opinion. Stay focused and keep going!

The negative things that people say about you is an indication of the direction of their path. No matter how it looks on the outside, it's killing them on the inside. Although it may seem like everything is against you, keep going, knowing that God takes care of His own.

When you understand your
purpose then you don't have
to say everything out loud.
Just continue to understand
it and trust the process.
Have FAITH.

Never let fear and anxiety
take you there; trust the
journey ahead. Show love
and be thankful.

God puts dreams in our hearts
and writes His destiny over our
lives. If we trust Him enough
and take Him at His Word,
we will journey towards the
fulfillment of our dreams.

Have faith. Keep the horizon
of a better day in mind and rise
with gratitude each new day.
Keep hustling and let your
dream become a reality. The
seed you plant today will bear a
harvest tomorrow.

Don't you ever let the doubters deter you from your blessing. You have worked too hard to even entertain doubt.

Just because you experience a setback, it doesn't mean that it's not going to happen. When you trust and believe in God, all things are possible.

It changed you because it challenged you. If it was easy, you would have walked all over it ungratefully.

You are stamped with the seal of approval of being enough. You are God's masterpiece; you don't need approval.

Everything you need is already lined up to fulfill your destiny. Your crooked place is straightening; your battles are being fought. Nothing can stop you. Get your fire back and stir up your faith.

Let your faith be strong and unshakeable. Let nothing stop you from being golden.

When God has assigned greatness in your life, there will always be people who want to find flaws to take down your greatness. Go out and be great anyway.

Remember: you are never going to keep everyone happy, so just run your race - shoulders back, chin up, and remember, you don't need their praise.

When your anointing matches your assignment, your victory will be sweatless.

Think high and rise above. You've got to be sure of yourself before you can be sure of anything else.

Just because you like something doesn't mean that it is good for you. Stop trying to entertain yourself with every nonsense that comes your way.

See the beauty in everything, because it's not what you look at that matters. It's about what you see. Be always in awe of the things you encounter and the tiny things in life will have so much meaning.

Sometimes you have to be your own superhero, because the ones you thought you couldn't live without, are living without you.

Happiness is a decision. Learn to focus on what you have rather than what you don't have. Keep winning and count your blessings.

Stop pouring your energy and time into the ones who always try to pull you down. Stop giving your power away. Know when to let go and when to hold on.

Today, choose to take charge of your life. Tell yourself that nothing will come in your way. The struggle is real, but with strength and determination you can achieve your goal. We are all winners.

The journey might not be easy, but we must learn to trust the process. Life is a challenge but press on and keep going; you can do it.

With determination, you can aim high. Always aim to be better than the person you were yesterday. Keep God first. You don't need to have everyone's validation to feel significant. Learn to accept your imperfection; learn to accept your true self. Be authentic; no one is perfect. After all, we all have our flaws. Just be you and own it.

Find peace within. You have the ability to do the things you love; do them to the best of your ability. Never let the beliefs of others deter you from your dream. People will always have something to say, no matter what. Learn to disregard the negative chaos. Use the strength and willpower that lies within you to motivate and give you that drive.

Stay on the highway and stop compromising your values. The greatness that's destined for your life doesn't need any validation. When God speaks, great things happen.

Embrace your beautiful season. You might just be seeing nothing but fog, but that big blessing is coming. Keep walking in your purpose and in your faith.